Praying With Authority and Power

STUDY GUIDE

*Taking Dominion Through Scriptural Prayers
and Prophetic Decrees*

Barbara L. Potts

Scripture quotations in this book are taken from the New King James Version, unless otherwise noted in the text. Any emphasis in Scripture quotes is the author's own. The following Bible translations were used: *The Open Bible*, New King James Version, copyright © 1997, 1990, 1985, 1983 by Thomas Nelson Publishers, Inc., *The Holy Bible*, New International Version (NIV), copyright © 1978 by New York International Bible Society, *The Amplified Bible*, Expanded Edition (AMP, TAB), copyright © 1987 by The Zondervan Corporation and The Lockman Foundation, *The First Scofield Reference Bible*, King James Version (KJV), copyright © 1986 by Barbour and Company, Inc., *The Message*, New Testament, Psalms, and Proverbs in Contemporary Language (MES), copyright © 1993, 1994, 1995 by Eugene H. Peterson, NavPress Publishing Group.

The editor has taken the liberty to respectfully acknowledge the Lord by capitalizing specific words relating to His Kingdom. These are: (the) Covenant, (the) Church, (the) Body (of Christ), Believers, the Blood (of the Lamb); and any pronouns referring to the Deity. McDougal Publishing also has chosen to *not* respectfully acknowledge satan by *not* capitalizing names relating to his kingdom, such as satan, allah, devil, and (the) enemy.

McDougal Publishing is a ministry of The McDougal Foundation, Inc., a Maryland nonprofit corporation dedicated to spreading the Gospel of the Lord Jesus Christ to as many people as possible in the shortest time possible.

Published by:

McDougal Publishing
P.O. Box 3595
Hagerstown, MD 21742-3595
www.mcdougalpublishing.com

ISBN 1-58158-091-6

Printed in the United States of America
For Worldwide Distribution

TABLE OF CONTENTS

INTRODUCTION

The book *Praying With Authority and Power* was written to instruct the reader in what the Bible says about the purpose and power of prayer, and motivate him or her to a deeper passion for, and commitment to, the discipline of intercession. The goal of this companion study guide is to encourage and empower personal and corporate prophetic intercession by providing a platform for group discussion and/or personal meditation on the principles and truths taught in the book.

KEY SCRIPTURE

One of the keys to powerful intercession is familiarity with the Word. Memorization is essential. Think of scripture memory as sharpening your sword. Every scripture you can pull out of the storehouse in your mind is a ready weapon. The Lord instructed us in John 15:7: "If you abide in Me, *and My words abide in you*, you will ask what you desire, and it shall be done for you." God's Word "abiding," or living, in us not only gives us authority in intercession, but directs our prayers to line up with God's will. We do not have what we ask in prayer, James said, because we ask "amiss," according to our own fleshly desires instead of asking according to God's will (James 4:3). But as we delight ourselves in the Lord and hide His Word in our hearts, we will have what we ask for, because it is His desire also. (See Psalm 37:4 and 1 John 5:14-15.) Therefore, it is important not only to know HOW to pray, but also to familiarize yourself with the Word, to be an effective intercessor. So, if you want to get the full benefit of this study guide, do memorize the "Key" scriptures that are highlighted—and seek to develop the discipline of scripture memorization. Many of the scriptures I hold in my prayer "arsenal" are there because of constant use. And if I can't recall the exact words of a verse or passage, I often know the scriptural location, and so my Bible is an essential reference tool as I pray.

Charles Spurgeon, recognized as one of the greatest preachers of all time, had this to say about the importance of Bible memorization (italics are mine):

"He hath said" (Hebrews 13:5). If we can only grasp these words by faith, we have an *all-conquering weapon in our hand*. What doubt will not be slain by this two-edged sword? What fear is there which shall not fall smitten with a deadly wound before this arrow from the bow of God's Covenant? Will not the distresses of life and the pangs of death; will not the corruptions within, and the snares without; will not the trials from above, and the temptations from beneath, all seem but light affliction, when we can hide ourselves beneath the bulwark of "He hath said?" Yes, *whether for delight in our quietude, or for strength in our conflict, "He hath said" must be our daily resort.* And this may teach us the extreme value of searching the Scriptures…. *Should you not, besides reading the Bible, store your memories richly with the promises of God?*…. Since "He hath said" is the source of all wisdom, and the fountain of all comfort, let it dwell in you richly, as "a well of water, springing up unto everlasting life." So shall you grow healthy, strong, and happy in the divine life.*

CHALLENGE

The main purpose of the *Challenge* at the end of each chapter is to apply some principle or discipline taught in the chapter. Taking up these challenges will serve to help develop a new prayer life, or strengthen an existing one. Some of the challenges also offer fresh insight to further empower the intercessor in the discipline of intercession.

*Charles Spurgeon, *Morning and Evening: Daily Readings* (Grand Rapids, MI: Zondervan, 1962),p.104.

Chapter One: THE CALL TO PRAY

1. What is prayer—and specifically, *intercession*?

2. What can we learn about intercession from Moses? Jeremiah? Jesus?

3. How can we know the will of God?

4. Read the Scripture references on pages 21-22 and discuss/consider the eight general truths of Scripture listed that can provide foundation for intercession.

KEY SCRIPTURE

Let us therefore come boldly to the throne of grace, that we may obtain mercy and find grace to help in time of need.   Hebrews 4:16

CHALLENGE

If you haven't already done so, make a personal commitment to devote at least 15 minutes at a certain time each day to begin to develop a prayer life, or longer to further develop an existing prayer life. This should be done between you and God. You will need His help, because as soon as you commit to prayer, expect to experience distractions and resistance. The devil isn't too concerned with your "good works" until you begin to pray. A praying Christian is his biggest threat. And he WILL throw everything at you to discourage you from praying.

Keep in mind that this is only a *beginning*. Too often people use prayer as a "last resort," when in reality prayer should be a *lifestyle*. There are different dimensions of prayer: focused intercessory prayer (in your *prayer closet*) and ongoing dialogue with God (as you walk through your day). Thus, your goal is to be in prayer "without ceasing" (1 Thessalonians 5:17). God is calling us to be in *spiritual connection* with Him at all times. The goal of intercessors at any level should be to live a *lifestyle* of prayer. Then talking with God will become as natural as breathing, and the Lord will become your delight (see Psalm 37:4).

Chapter Two: THE ARMOR OF GOD

1. In spiritual warfare, who is our enemy?

2. What is the most important piece of spiritual armor?—Why?

3. What is the significance of the mind as the "window to the soul"?—What does the *helmet of salvation* do?

4. What is the function of the *breastplate of righteousness*?—What makes us righteous?

5. What is the function of the *girdle of truth?*—How does this protect us?

6. What is the power behind the *gospel of peace?*—What is the power of unforgiveness, and how does it hinder us?

7. According to Hebrews 4:12, what two things does the Word of God do?—What effect does the *sword of the spirit* have against the enemy in intercession?

8. What is the *armor of light?*—How does it help us?

9. What is the purpose of the armor of God?—What is the enemy always doing?—Who gives us strength to stand and to conquer?

For we do not wrestle against flesh and blood, but against principalities, against the rulers of the darkness of this age, against spiritual hosts of wickedness in the heavenly places. Ephesians 6:12

CHALLENGE

During your prayer time each day, ask the Lord to specifically strengthen each piece of your spiritual armor. (See pages 216-220 in the book.) And then don't be surprised when you encounter tests:

- to purify your thinking (helmet)
- to strengthen your faith (shield)
- to teach you truth (girdle, belt)
- to call you to righteous living (breastplate)
- to "live peaceably with all men" (shoes)
- to learn the veracity of the Word of God (sword)

Instead of struggling against trials and tribulations, practice having the mindset of James 1:2-4:

My brethren, count it all joy when you fall into various trials, knowing that the testing of your faith produces patience. But let patience have its perfect work, that you may be perfect and complete, lacking nothing.

For a further expansion of the interworking of trials and grace, consider again the wise words of Charles Spurgeon (italics are mine):

If none of God's saints were poor and tried, we should not know half so well the consolations of divine grace. When we find the wanderer who has no where to lay his head, who yet can say, "Still I will trust in the Lord;" when we see the pauper starving on bread and water, who still glories in Jesus; when we see the bereaved widow overwhelmed in affliction, and yet having faith in Christ, Oh! What honor it reflects on the Gospel. *God's grace is illustrated and magnified in the poverty and trials of believers.* Saints bear up under every discouragement, believing that all things work together for their good, and that out of apparent evils a real blessing shall ultimately spring. *This patience of the saints proves the power of divine grace.* The masterworks of God are those men who stand in the midst of difficulties, steadfast, unmovable,…confident in victory. *He who would glorify his God must set his account upon meeting with many trials. If, then, yours be a much-tried path, rejoice in it, because you will the better show forth the all-sufficient grace of God.**

*Charles Spurgeon, Morning and Evening: Daily Readings (Grand Rapids, MI: Zondervan, 1962), p.128.

Chapter Three: THE BELIEVER'S STANDING IN CHRIST: TAKING DOMINION

1. What is the ultimate goal of all prayer?

2. What is man's place within the created realm?

3. What was man's original role in the Garden?—How did he lose his place of authority?

4. What are the two kingdoms that men can live in, as described in Ephesians 2:1-6? What are the characteristics of the citizens of each?—Who is the "prince of the power of the air"?

5. What is the *Kingdom of God?*—What are the two dimensions of the *Kingdom of God?*—How do we become part of the Kingdom of God?—How is God's Kingdom formed in us?

6. How did man regain dominion in the earth?—Describe the Believer's position of authority in Christ according to Ephesians 1:20 and 2:6.—What does it mean to be "translated" into the Kingdom of God? What are the benefits of this?

7. What gives Believers authority to command demons?

8. How does Revelation 12:11 say that we overcome the devil?—What is the "word of our testimony"?

9. Who is the "Bride of Christ"?—What gives her favor with the King, and thus authority in intercession?

10. Who will sit with Christ on His throne?—What will be the main characteristic of this group?

11. Put yourself into Revelation 3:20.—How would you respond to the Lord's knocking?

KEY SCRIPTURE

I give you the authority to trample on serpents and scorpions [pictures of demonic spirits], *and over all the power of the enemy, and nothing shall by any means hurt you.*   Luke 10:19

CHALLENGE

1. Consider an area or situation in your life where you have relinquished your place of dominion to the enemy through unconfessed sin, lack of faith, or ignorance. Begin to take back the ground you have lost:
    *   Confess your sin to God (see 1 John 1:9)
    *   Ask God to help you in your weakness (see 2 Corinthians 12:9)
    *   Begin to take the authority you have been given as a Blood Covenant child of God (see Luke 10:19) by exercising the "word of your testimony" over the situation (Examples: Isaiah 54:17, Colossians 2:15, Romans 8:37, 2 Timothy 1:7).

2. Reread Jeanne Guyon's description of *abandonment* on pages 39-40. How does this stir your heart?—Respond to the Lord's prompting.

Chapter Four: PREVAILING IN PRAYER

1. What does Charles Finney say is essential to prevail in prayer?—Hence, what is the first step toward God in prayer?

2. What is the basis of our confidence to approach the throne of grace?

3. What essential heart attitude is identified in 1 Peter 5:5-7?

4. Jesus instructed His disciples in Mark 11:24 that "whatever things you ask when you pray, _____, and you will have them."

5. What was unique about Peter's prayer over the lame man in Acts 3:6?—What happened as a result?—In this scenario, who had *faith*: the man who was healed or Peter, who prayed?—What is the message here for the intercessor?

6. What is a common prayer pitfall?—How can one guard against this?

7. What does John 15:7 tell the intercessor about praying according to God's will?

8. Why was David described by God as a "man after His own heart"?—What is the relationship between intimacy with God and spiritual authority?—If you put yourself into the vision of the dance floor, how would your dancing appear to the observer?

9. What two things does obedience to God accomplish?

10. What are the life lessons in the parable in Luke 18:1-8 and in the admonition in Matthew 7:7-8?

11. What two dynamics can prevent immediate answers to faith-filled prayers?

12. What is the "attitude of advancement," and how does it open the door to answered prayer?

13. What five personal spiritual benefits come as a result of prayer—other than the answers we seek?—Can you think of times when you have experienced any of these benefits?

14. How does prayer affect the heavenly realm?—What three arenas of dominion do angels exercise authority over?—What are the main ministry activities of angels?

KEY SCRIPTURE

If you abide in Me, and My words abide in you, you will ask what you desire, and it shall be done for you.   John 15:7

CHALLENGE

Create your own "prayer altar"—your place of meeting with God each day. Be sure to incorporate worship and praise, meditation (on a scripture verse or passage), thanksgiving and confession before you begin to raise your petitions. Familiarize yourself with the psalms, and gradually make some verses your "own" to pray back to God. Don't be in a hurry, but "delight yourself in the Lord"—for *He* then delights to give you the "desires of your heart" (Psalm 37:4).

If you already have a prayer routine established, purpose to spend even *more* time in worship and communion with the Lover of your soul, seeking with renewed passion the intimacy of the Bride.

Chapter Five: PROPHETIC INTERCESSION

1. What is *prophetic intercession*?

2. "God has limited His activity in the lives of men based on
   _____ ."

3. What is the main work of the devil?

4. What authority do Believers have in prayer according to Luke 10:19?

5. What is the prophetic scripture that reveals God's intention to empower His Church to fulfill the Great Commission?—What was the disciples' response to this word from God that gives us direction in prayer today?

6. What three prayer strategies did Moses use when he was interceding for rebellious Israel that we can use today?

7. What gave Amos understanding about how to pray for Israel?—What does this tell us about how God can generate intercession in His people today?

8. What does Ezekiel 22:30-31 tell us about the potential power of intercession?

9. Jonah was in a "tight place" because of disobedience. What does his prayer reveal about his change of heart?—What direction does this give the intercessor?

Now this is the confidence that we have in Him, that if we ask any-thing according to His will, He hears us. And if we know that He hears us, whatever we ask, we know that we have the petitions that we have asked of Him.   1 John 5:14-15

CHALLENGE

Consider a particular situation that you have been anxious about, or praying over. Ask the Lord to give you a word from Scripture that you can begin to pray over the situation. For example, if there is a need for some sort of provision—financial, job or other—Philippians 4:19 is a Covenant promise that God's children can draw from: *"And my God shall supply all your need according to His riches in glory by Christ Jesus."* Think of Covenant promises of God as blank checks that are available to be cashed in Heaven through prayer. Charles Spurgeon had this to say about declaring God's promises (italics are mine):

> Nothing pleases our Lord better than to see His promises put in circulation....*We glorify God when we plead His promises.* Our heavenly Banker loves to cash in His own notes. Never let the promise rest. Draw the word of promise out of its scabbard, and use it with holy violence.... God loves to hear the loud outcries of needy souls. It is His delight to bestow favors. He is more ready to hear than you are to ask.... *It is God's nature to keep His promises.**

* Charles Spurgeon, *Morning and Evening: Daily Readings* (Grand Rapids, MI: Zondervan, 1962), p. 30.

Chapter Six: MAKING DECREES: GOVERNMENTAL AUTHORITY

1. What is *governmental authority?*—What power does this give us with God over the created realm?

2. What are the progressions of government in the Kingdom of God?

3. How should scriptures like Isaiah 60:1-3 and Revelation 11:15 motivate us to pray?

4. What other principle does the *key of David* work synergistically with?—How?

5. What is the significance of the *house of David* in Isaiah 22:22?

6. What does the "key" represent in Isaiah 22:22?

7. What does Isaiah 22:22 tell us about the governmental authority that has been released to us?—"The *key of the house of David* gives us_____ to occupy by_____."

8. What prayer models (how one can pray) are highlighted in the examples of Jesus and Mary?

9. How do we bring our need into alignment with God's provision?

10. What important key to prevailing in prayer does Job 22:23-28 highlight?

11. According to Esther 8:8, what gives the decree authority?—What authority in prayer do Isaiah 22:22 and Esther 8:8 together give the intercessor?—What seals the spiritual doors in this decree?

12. What is the caution in confronting the enemy?—What is our work and what is God's?

The key of the house of David I will lay on his shoulder; so he shall open, and no one shall shut; and he shall shut, and no one shall open.

Isaiah 22:22

CHALLENGE

Think of a situation in your life where the enemy has gained access to harass, oppress or hinder you or a family member. Then, using your authority from Isaiah 22:22 and Esther 8:8, write a decree to *close* doors in the spirit realm to the demonic activity, applying the Blood of the Lamb over the doorposts and lintels, and to *open* the door to God's restoration work.

As you consider the call of the intercessor into spiritual warfare, let the inspiring words of Charles Spurgeon stir your heart to overcoming faith for the battle:

Warrior, fighting under the banner of the Lord Jesus, observe this verse with holy joy:

There fell down many slain, because the war was of God.

1 Chronicles 5:22

For as it was in the days of old, so it is now: *if the war be of God the victory is sure.* Quail not before superior numbers, shrink not from difficulties or impossibilities, flinch not at wounds or death, *smite with the two-edged sword of the Spirit, and the slain shall lie in heaps.* The battle is the Lord's and *He will deliver His enemies into our hands.* With steadfast foot, strong hand, dauntless heart, and flaming zeal, rush to the conflict, and the hosts of evil shall fly like chaff before the gale.*

*Charles Spurgeon, *Morning and Evening: Daily Readings* (Grand Rapids, Michigan: Zondervan, 1962), p.320

Praying With Authority and Power Study Guide

Chapter Seven: THE POWER OF THE BLOOD AND THE NAME OF JESUS

1. What is the foundation of our authority and power in prayer?

2. What does the Blood of the Covenant represent/provide for Believers?

3. What do Romans 8:17, Luke 10:19 and John 14:12 tell us about the spiritual authority of the Believer?

4. If Jesus triumphed over all the powers of darkness by the Blood of His cross, how do they continue to exert influence over men and nations?

5. Why is praying a *Blood covering* a strategic weapon in spiritual warfare?

6. What does the testimony of Mahesh Chavda show us about spiritual authority?

7. What is the significance of the name of Jesus that requires us to pray in His name?

8. What access does the authority of His name give Believers according to the scriptures at the top of page 77?

9. Read Colossians 1:15-19.—What validity does this give to the authority of Christ?

10. To what did Peter attribute the lame man's healing in Acts 3:16?—
How does this help us to pray?

11. According to Acts 4:29-30, how did the servants of Jesus perform signs
and wonders?

12. What is it that causes evil spirits to recognize legal authority?

KEY SCRIPTURE

Having disarmed *principalities and powers*, [Jesus] *made a public spectacle of them*, triumphing over *them in* [the cross].

Colossians 2:15

CHALLENGE

To strengthen your faith in the power of the Blood, using a concordance, prayerfully research all the New Testament references to the Blood of Jesus. As you meditate, let the Holy Spirit bring fresh revelation on what your Savior has purchased for you. In the words of Andrew Murray, a classic and prolific Christian writer: "The believer who desires to understand completely the *blessed power of the Blood* must submit entirely to the teaching of the Word through the Holy Spirit in private."* Then, remember to declare often as you pray that **the Blood of the Lamb of God, Jesus Christ, *has triumphed over and continues to prevail against* all the powers of darkness and evil!**

*Andrew Murray, *The Blood of the Cross* (New Kensington, PA: Whitaker House, 1981), p. 56.

Chapter Eight: PRAYING THE NEWS/HEADLINES

1. What are the three strategies used in the sample decree made over Kandahar?

2. What does the example of the hurricane reveal to us as intercessors concerning the relationship between spiritual and natural phenomena?— How did the prayer concerning the hurricane threat appeal to God?

3. What does Joseph's experience teach us about trusting God?

4. What is a good way to pray when tragic things, or things we don't understand, happen?

Be anxious for nothing, but in everything, by prayer and supplication, with thanksgiving, let your requests be made known to God; and the peace of God, which surpasses all understanding, will guard your hearts and minds through Christ Jesus. Philippians 4:6

CHALLENGE

Begin to practice reading the news from a "prayer" perspective. That is, thank God for good news, and intercede over the bad. Laying hands on a photograph while making decrees is a powerful way to respond to current events. This can be very simple, such as calling leaders to wisdom, and criminals to salvation. Ask God to show you an article/situation in the news that He wants you to mount a prolonged prayer campaign over, and prayerfully begin to craft a decree for the situation.

Chapter Nine: BINDING AND LOOSING

1. What are the *keys of the Kingdom?*

2. According to Ms. Savard, what does Christ's giving of these "keys" represent?

3. Basically, what does the strategy of "binding and loosing" involve?

4. What is a *stronghold?*—What are some things which cause the erecting of strongholds?—What is their effect on a person?

5. What are the two sides of "binding," and how do they work?

6. What is the typical pattern of how a stronghold is erected?

7. What pulls down strongholds?—How does this work?

8. Where are personal spiritual battles waged?—What must be done to protect ourselves in this battle?

9. Describe the powerful way to pray the "binding and loosing" strategy.

And I will give you the keys of the kingdom of heaven, and whatever you bind on earth will be bound in heaven, and whatever you loose on earth will be loosed in heaven. Matthew 16:19

CHALLENGE

The following declaration to set the captives free utilizes the *keys of the Kingdom* plus the *Blood of Jesus* and the *key of the house of David*. Begin to pray this over someone you know, and watch for God to move in their life to set them free:

In the name of Jesus Christ, I bind _____'s body, soul and spirit to the will and purposes of God for his/her life. I bind him/her to the truth and to the Blood of Jesus. I bind his/her mind to the mind of Christ, that the very thoughts, feelings and purposes of His heart would be within his/her thoughts. I bind his/her feet to the paths of righteousness, that his/her steps would be steady and sure in the calling that is on his/her life. I bind him/her to the work of the cross with all of its mercy, grace, love, forgiveness and dying to self. I bind him/her to the work of the Resurrection, with all of its overcoming faith, abundant life and health, prosperity and victory. I bind him/her to a passion for Jesus and compassion for the Body of Christ. I bind him/her to wisdom, knowledge, true discernment and all the gifts of the Spirit. I bind him/her to faith, humility, godly character and all the fruit of the Spirit.

Binding every thought captive to Christ (see 2 Corinthians 10:5), I loose every old, wrong and ungodly pattern of thinking, attitude, idea, desire, belief, motivation, habit and behavior from _____. I tear down and destroy every stronghold associated with these things. I loose any stronghold in his/her life that has been justifying and protecting any sinful, damaging behavior. I loose the strongholds of unforgiveness, fear, distrust, pride, self-sufficiency and rebellion from him/her.

I loose the power and effects of all deceptions and lies from _____. I loose the effects of every seducing spirit that has found access into his/her mind... (name them, if you know them) I close the doors of access the enemy has used, and apply the Blood of the Lamb over the lintels and doorposts in the spirit realm so that the death angel may not enter. I speak to his/her spiritual and physical (when drug/alcohol abuse is present) livers and declare them to be purified by the Blood of the Lamb, cleansing them from every defilement and restoring him/her to a healthy body and a pure conscience. I loose the confusion and blindness of the god of this world from his/her mind that has kept him/her from seeing the truth of the Gospel of Jesus Christ. I call forth every precious word of Scripture that has ever entered into his/her mind and heart, that it would rise up in power within him/her.

In the name of Jesus, I loose every demonic hindrance and influence over _____ body, mind and spirit. I uproot the unrighteous seed, with its generational curses and familiar spirits, and I cut off any unhealthy soul ties. And I sow the righteous seed, that it might bring forth the fruits of righteousness (see Hebrews 3:18) and love: I call forth kindness, patience, generosity, humility, courtesy, selflessness, good temper, guilelessness and sincerity (see 1 Corinthians 13:4-8).

I loose the power and effects of any harsh or hard words (or word curses) spoken to, about or by _____. I loose all generational bondages and associated strongholds from him/her. I loose all effects and bondages from him/her that may have been caused by mistakes that I have made, or from any pain or woundedness incurred during childhood. Father, in the name of Jesus, I destroy generational bondages of any kind from mistakes made at any point between generations. I destroy them right here, right now. They will not bind and curse any more members of this family. I loose the enemy's influence over every part of his/her body, soul and spirit. I loose him/her from all works, influences and lusts of the flesh, including defeat, lack, unforgiveness, infirmity, confusion, doubt, fear and control.

I bind and loose these things in Jesus' name, for He has given me the keys and the authority to do so. I thank You, Lord, for everything that You have allowed to come into _____'s life for the purpose of strengthening his/her faith and revealing Your glory. I ask You to pour Your anointing of grace upon her/him now so that every bondage may be destroyed! Thank You, Lord, for the truth that sets the captives free! Amen!*

I need to mention here what I believe is a common misinterpretation and, thus, misuse, of a particular scripture. The scripture appears twice in the gospels, and it refers to "binding the strong man":

- Luke 11:22: *"But when a stronger than he comes upon him and overcomes him, he takes from him all his armor in which he trusted, and divides his spoils."*
- Matthew 12:29: *"Or how can one enter a strong man's house and plunder his goods, unless he first binds the strong man?"*

In these passages Jesus' authority is being challenged by the Pharisees who say that His power comes from the devil. Jesus is saying here that, far from operating out of demonic power, HE, Almighty God incarnate, is the "stronger" One who "overcomes" and "binds the strong man" and *plunders the entire demonic kingdom.* By casting out demons and delivering people of mental and physical sicknesses, He was plundering the devil's "goods" (those in bondage) and taking the "spoils" (lost souls) for Himself.

The error that I see, and have operated in myself in the past, is in interpreting this as license for Believers to "bind" the devil. In the first place, as I point out on page 91, satan will not truly be "bound" until he is bound and cast into the bottomless pit by the angel of God for one thousand years. Secondly, I believe that Scripture delegates our authority over satan directly through the *Blood of the Lamb* (Revelation 12:11)—and that is the weapon we wield: *The Blood of Jesus Christ, the Lamb of God, has triumphed over the devil and continues to prevail against him* (See Colossians 2:15). Hence, I do not "bind" the devil in spiritual warfare. Following Jesus' example, I rebuke and cast out demons (this effectively binds the devil's power) and *enforce the triumph of Christ over the powers of darkness* according to Colossians 2:15. For indeed, all things were created by Him and for Him: He reigns supreme over ALL and through Him ALL things consist. (See Colossians 1:15-18).

As intercessors, we must be wise to understand what our God-given authority allows us to do. I repeat: *The battle is the Lord's.* Our function is to stand, declare, and petition. God's work is to direct the spiritual warfare in the heavenlies (per our prayers), pull down strongholds, and set the captives free.

---

* Adapted from Liberty Savard, *Shattering Your Strongholds* (North Brunswick, NJ: Bridge-Logos Publishers, 1998), p. 171-172.

Chapter Ten: PROPHETIC IDENTIFICATION

1. How did Jesus use *prophetic identification*?

2. How can we, as intercessors, identify with the woman in Luke 18?

3. How is the grace of Abimelech used in praying for President George W. Bush?

4. How can ancient biblical prophetic scriptures be relevant to current events?

So shall My word be that goes forth from My mouth; it shall not return to Me void, but it shall accomplish what I please, and it shall prosper in the thing for which I sent it.   Isaiah 55:11

CHALLENGE

Luke 15:11-32 recounts the story of the *prodigal son,* who left his father's house with all his inheritance and squandered it on riotous living. Later he "came to himself" and returned to his father in repentance: "Father, I have sinned against heaven and in your sight." He was restored completely to his father and his previous life with great fanfare and celebration: "It was right that we should make merry and be glad, for your brother was dead and is alive again, and was lost and is found."—Then, using the strategy of *prophetic identification,* think of a person you know who is like the prodigal son, having left his "(heavenly) father's house," that is, his Christian upbringing, and who needs to be restored. Then pray that he, like the prodigal, would "come to himself" and return (repent), and that God would completely restore him to his family and his (spiritual) inheritance.

Chapter Eleven: THE PRAYER OF AGREEMENT

1. Read Daniel 2:1-19 to see how the *prayer of agreement* averted disaster in the lives of Daniel and his companions, and in the lives of all the wise men of Babylon.

2. What is the *key* in the Old Testament mathematical model for the *prayer of agreement?*

3. Read the "Song of Moses" in Deuteronomy 32. In verse 30, how could judgment be a blessing?—Why is judgment sometimes necessary, even for God's people?—Is this something that our nation could face in the future if we don't turn back to God?—As in the time of Daniel and the Israelites, could we avert judgment through the prayer of agreement? The decrees in Chapter Sixteen of this book are a foundation for praying in agreement for this very thing.

4. How does the agreement on the natural field of battle translate into spiritual warfare?

5. What does it really mean to "agree" in prayer?

KEY SCRIPTURE

Again I say to you that if two of you agree on earth concerning anything that they ask, it will be done for them by My Father in heaven. For where two or three are gathered together in My name, I am there in the midst of them. Matthew 18:19-20

CHALLENGE

If you don't already have one, find a prayer partner whom you can pray regularly *in agreement* with. All issues or needs have a solution in Scripture. Be sure that what you are asking for lines up with God's Word. And keep in mind that most often the "solution" involves waiting. But know that as you submit your petitions to God in prayer, He *will* work all things out for your ultimate good (see Romans 8:28).

Chapter Twelve: THE POWER OF PRAISE, WORSHIP AND COMMUNION

1. Read 2 Chronicles 20:1-30 concerning Judah's battle with Moab and Ammon.

   - What was Jehoshaphat's response when he heard the news about the imminent threat of attack? (verse 3)

   - What does he remind the Lord of in verses 7-9 and 11?

   - What truth is revealed in verse 15 that is significant to the intercessor?

   - What was the strategy that routed the enemy in verses 21-22?

   - What did the people of Judah get out of the battle besides victory? (verse 25)—This is a reality in spiritual warfare as well. God will return the spoil that the devil has stolen from us. He is in the restoration "business" (see Joel 2:12-27).

- What did the people do when the victory was complete? (verse 28)

2. What does Acts 16:25-26 teach the intercessor about the effects of praise in the spiritual realm?

3. Why do we need to praise God, and what personal benefits do we derive from this?

4. What does praise and worship do to the kingdom of darkness?

5. What is pictured in Revelation 5:8, and how is this significant to the intercessor?

6. "The celebration of the Body and Blood of our Lord, is an intimate act of worship which _____

   _____."

7. From the perspective of intercession, what two powerful things does the atoning sacrifice of Jesus provide for us?

KEY SCRIPTURE

Delight yourself also in the LORD and He shall give you the desires of your heart.   Psalm 37:4

CHALLENGE

Praise (extolling God for the great things He has done) and Communion are both ways to worship the Lord. But worship goes beyond singing, dancing, and praying. Expanding on this theme of worship, Romans 12:1 (NIV) teaches that true worship should involve the offering of one's *whole life:*

I urge you, therefore, brothers, in view of God's mercy, to offer your bodies as living sacrifices, *holy and pleasing to God—which is your spiritual worship.*

Our "spiritual worship" here is the offering of our bodies as "*living* sacrifices" unto God—or, that *all* we do, think and say would be done to *please and honor Him.* Worship shouldn't stop when we leave our *altar of prayer.* Keeping this in mind, make a conscious effort each morning to offer yourself—your body, your *life*—as a "living sacrifice" to the glory and purposes of God. Determine to "discipline your body and bring it into subjection" (1 Corinthians 9:27) to your spirit by *binding* your mind, will and emotions to the will and purposes of God. Then determine to live *for Him*, that your life would be an offering to His praise and glory!

Chapter Thirteen: THE POWER OF FASTING

1. "We cannot be _____-led and _____-driven people at the same time."

2. What are the characteristics of the flesh that hinder our spiritual development?—How does fasting help this situation?

3. What should the *personal faith declaration* of every serious intercessor be?—Why? (according to Matthew 16:24)

4. Read and study the account of the wilderness temptation of Jesus in Luke 4:1-14.

   • Who led Jesus into the wilderness?—Why?—What did Jesus need that He didn't already have? (Compare the activity of the Spirit in verses 1 and 14.)—If Jesus benefited from this experience, do you think the Holy Spirit would lead you into a "wilderness" experience also?—Have you ever *had* such an experience? (If so, what did you gain from it?)

- What in Jesus did the devil appeal to in verses 3 and 6? (hint: something that fasting chastens)

- How did Jesus respond to the devil's temptations?—What lesson does this teach the intercessor?

- How did the devil change his strategy in verses 9 through 11?— What do verses 9 and 10 tell us about the devil?—Note: The devil will always seek to make us doubt the veracity of God's Word, because he knows its power. But can he use the Word of God with any authority?

- What does verse 13 tell us about the activity of the devil?

- In this passage, what things do you see that fasting accomplished?

5. As we crucify the flesh, what happens to our spirit man?

6. "Our *inadequacy* is God's _____."
   What makes us strong according to John 3:30 and 2 Corinthians 12:9-10?—As an intercessor, how does this reality make you feel?

7. What reason to fast was exemplified in the account of Phinehas and the tribes of Israel?

8. What did fasting accomplish during the period of the Judges (1 Samuel 7:3-6) when Israel was being threatened by the Philistines?

9. How did fasting help Ahab in 1 Kings 21?

10. Why did David think that his fasting would bring his illegitimate child back to life?—What did David do when the child died?—What lesson is this to the intercessor?

11. What door did fasting open for Nehemiah?—How was he received by the king?

12. What does the account of the demon-possessed men of the Gergesenes in Matthew 8:28-34 reveal about the authority of the Spirit-filled Believer?

13. Read the account of the demon-possessed boy in Mark 9:14-29.—What does it tell us about the relationship between prayer and fasting?—What other important dynamic of prevailing prayer is highlighted by Jesus in verses 19 and 23?

KEY SCRIPTURE

I am crucified with Christ: nevertheless I live; yet not I, but Christ liveth in me: and the life which I now live in the flesh I live by the faith of the Son of God, who loved me, and gave himself for me.

Galatians 2:20, KJV

CHALLENGE

Fasting is a spiritual *discipline*. And it takes time and practice to develop this discipline. But like I used to tell my children: If you desire to fast (or do anything difficult that pleases the Lord), you can—just use your *will-power:*

Willpower = *my* will + *God's* power.

If you have never developed this discipline, begin small. For instance, fast one meal a day at first, and build. Pray and ask the Lord what He would have you fast for. It might be a personal situation, salvation or healing for someone else, or possibly just to sharpen your spiritual senses or to get closer to Him. Then pick a day of the week and begin to fast regularly on that day as you pray over the need/desire. Then expect to see results! This is faith which pleases and honors God. (See Hebrews 11:6.) When you get there, here are a few practical suggestions for extended fasting:

1. Eat lightly the day before you begin your fast.
2. Always drink a lot of water, before and during your fast.
3. Avoid high-sugar fruit juices.—V-8 or cranberry juice are better.
4. Because I can't afford to lose much weight, I use a protein powder in soy milk twice a day when fasting for long periods.
5. Try to get more sleep than usual.—You will need it.
6. Continue regular mild exercise, like walking.—rest when you need to.
7. Declare the fasting scriptures at the end of the chapter when you feel hungry.—I especially like the one in Job 23:12: "I have esteemed the words of His mouth more than my necessary food."
8. Spend more time in prayer and meditation. Spend the time you would be feeding your body "eating" the *meat* of God's Word.
9. Celebrate Communion at home in your prayer closet before you begin your day, if you are comfortable doing this outside of your church.—This is very strengthening spiritually and physically.

If you have already developed a fasting discipline, let God stretch you beyond what you have previously experienced. Unless we allow ourselves to be stretched beyond our own abilities (or comfort zones), we will never know the power of God in our lives.

Chapter Fourteen: THE POWER OF REPENTANCE AND TRAVAIL

1. According to 2 Chronicles 7:14, what must God's people do to bring healing to the land?—What direction does this give to us as intercessors?

2. What saved Nineveh?—What does this show us about the character of God?

3. How will the *Kingdom of God* come to the earth, and how does repentance fit into this scenario?

4. Why had the Lord pronounced judgment on Israel in Jeremiah 9:13-14?—Do you think our nation is any different today?—What averted disaster?—What is the purpose of travail in verse 18?—How then should we pray?

5. What brought forth the outbreak of revival in Albany and Pensacola?

6. What should our response be to the current prevailing prophetic message to the Church concerning revival?

CHALLENGE

Heretofore, you may have only experienced praying for personal needs. Begin to purpose spending some of your daily prayer time focused on praying for our nation, using the information in this chapter.

Seasoned intercessors, refresh your commitment to praying daily for revival.

Chapter Fifteen: THE POWER OF PRAYING IN THE HOLY SPIRIT

1. Who is the "Helper"?—What is His work?

2. What is the "Promise of the Father"?— What is the purpose of this Holy Spirit experience?

3. What are the three main functions of *tongues*? — Why do we need help in prayer?

   What is the instruction given in Jude 20?

4. What other *power* and *revelatory* gifts are listed in 1 Corinthians 12:7-10? —What should be the focus of these gifts in corporate worship? —What is the admonition of Paul to the Church in 1 Corinthians 14:39?

5. Read Acts 8:14-17 — What is the difference indicated here between "water" baptism (the baptism of John) and the Holy Spirit baptism?

6. According to Acts 10:44-48, who is the Holy Spirit Baptism given to? —What was the evidence of having received the Baptism?

7. According to Acts 19:2-6, what can the Baptism experience coincide with?

8. What was the prophet Joel speaking about in Joel 2:28-32?

9. "The Baptism in the Holy Spirit was given by God to His Church, His Body, so we can_____."

KEY SCRIPTURE

"I indeed baptize you with water unto repentance, but He who is coming after me is mightier than I, whose sandals I am not worthy to carry, He will baptize you with the Holy Spirit and fire."

Matthew 3:11

CHALLENGE

We see from this chapter that the *Baptism in the Holy Spirit* is given for power in service, for power in prayer, and for personal edification. If you have never received this empowerment, and would like to, it is very simple to do. As has been revealed through the Scriptures just presented, Jesus is the *Baptizer.* And just as you asked Him as Savior to save you, you ask Him as Baptizer to baptize you. And then, just like salvation, believe by faith that you have received.

During your devotional time, prayerfully meditate over the Scriptures in this chapter. Then ask Jesus to baptize you with His Holy Spirit and begin to praise the Him in song or words, but don't use English—Let the Spirit fill your mouth. The evidence of speaking in tongues may come immediately, in fullness, or it may take a while, a few words at a time. I prayed and waited for a year for my prayer language to manifest. But my son received his all at once when he first sought the Lord. The "how" and "when" experience is different for each person. But know that the Baptism is available to all Believers who ask.

If you already have a prayer language, understand that the more you use it, the more it will expand. Use it more often in intercession and devotion. Even use it in ways you may not have tried before, such as:

- If you need wisdom or insight when struggling with a challenge or a practical problem.
- To sing a "spirit" song (see Ephesians 5:19) to the Lord.
- When observing a confrontational, or potentially dangerous situation.
- ANYTIME you don't know how to pray.

Remember that there are NINE gifts of the Holy Spirit associated with the Baptism experience. Paul admonished the Church to "*earnestly desire the best gifts*"…and "*desire spiritual gifts*, but especially that you may prophesy." (1 Corinthians 12:31 and 14:1) Don't rest content with whatever gift(s) you may have, but earnestly seek more, that you may mature in the character of Jesus your Lord, build the Kingdom, and glorify Him in even greater measure.

Chapter Sixteen: THE CHURCH

1. What is the primary condition necessary to bring revival to this (or any) nation?

2. How is Revelation 3:16-19 a picture of the Church today?—What is God's remedy?—What is the significance of gold, white garments and eye salve?

3. What does the condition of *lukewarmness* reveal about the focus of one's life?—How does this compare with the command in Matthew 22:37-38?

4. What are the three spiritual forces identified as the "unholy trinity"?

- Who was *Jezebel,* historically?—Read 1 Kings 21 to witness her wicked, conniving ways.—How does the *spirit of Jezebel* manifest against God's people today?—Can you think of examples of this spiritual activity that you have seen or experienced?

- What does the name *Balaam* mean, and who was he, historically?— Read Numbers 22-24 to see how he operated out of greed, covetousness and selfishness.— How does the *spirit of Balaam* operate in the Church today?—Can you think of examples of this spiritual activity?

- What is the manifestation, or evidence, of the *pharisee spirit* in the Church today?—How does *legalism* kill?—Read Matthew 23 to see how Jesus characterized the Pharisees of His day.— How have you observed this spirit at work seeking to kill genuine spiritual life in the Church today?

5. What is making the Body of Christ "sick"?

6. What are "functional" gifts, and what is their purpose?—How are they different from "spiritual" gifts?

7. What is necessary for the Body to come into proper alignment?—What is the measure, or indicator, of the indwelling Christ in His Body?

8. What will be God's *end-time* witness to the world?

9. What ungodly attitude does the Church need to repent of, and what revelation does she need concerning this?

KEY SCRIPTURE

...that they may all be one, as You, Father, are in Me, and I in You; that they also may be one in Us, that the world may believe that You sent Me...and have loved them as You have loved Me.

John 17:21 and 23—Jesus' prayer for the Church

CHALLENGE

Jesus said that the *"first and great commandment"* is to *"love the LORD your God with all your heart, with all your soul, and with all your mind"* (Matthew 22:37-38). "And the second is like it: *'You shall love your neighbor as your-self'* " (verse 39). Jesus also said, "If you love Me, keep My command-ments" (John 14:15).

1. Reread the prayer-poem on pages 38-39. What can you do personally toward this goal of loving the Lord totally, with your *whole* being? Keep in mind that how much *time* you spend with a person is a measure of your love for them.

2. Purpose to show God's love toward someone in your life who is "hard" to love—not because you *feel* like it, but because the Lord *requires* it.— Some suggestions:

    *   *"A **soft answer** turns away wrath"* (Proverbs 15:1).

    *   *"**Bless** those who curse you, and **pray** for those who spitefully use you"* (Luke 6:28).

    *   *"**Love** your enemies, **do good**, and **lend**, hoping for nothing in return"* (Luke 6:35).

    *   ***Forgive*** "seventy times seven" (Matthew 18:22).— *"If you do not for-give men their trespasses, neither will your* [heavenly] *Father forgive your trespasses"* (Matthew 6:15).

Chapter Seventeen: THE UNITED STATES

1. What is foundational to our intercession for the United States?—Why?

2. According to Ezekiel 22:30, what is God's desire toward a wayward nation?

3. What specific sins in Isaiah 59 are endemic to our nation?

4. What do Ezekiel 14:6 and Joel 2:13 say will bring the revival we need?—

   Read Psalm 81:
   • What is the command of God in verses 8-9?—What "foreign gods" do we worship in America?

- What is Israel's response in verse 11?—What is the evidence that God's people in our nation are not heeding His plea to turn back to Him?

- What is God's response in verse 12?—What is the evidence in our nation that God has let us go our own way?

- What is God longing to do in verses 14-16?—What changes do you think we would see in this nation if God's people began to repent?

5. What prayer strategies can the intercessor glean from Moses (Exodus 32) and Daniel (Daniel 9) to help pray for our nation?—Look for these and other points (pleas for mercy, forgiveness, cleansing, revelation, and so forth) in the *Prayer for the United States*.

6. Why, according to Romans 11 has Israel been blinded to seeing Jesus as the Messiah?—What is the shared destiny of Israel and the United States? (See Ephesians 2:13-16.)—What does God's Covenant guarantee will be restored to Israel?—What direction does Joel 3:2 give to our leaders concerning Israel?—Is relinquishing any part of Israel's land an option in the peace process?—Is it even possible for men to negotiate peace for Israel?

7. According to 1 Timothy 2:2 and 4, why should we pray for all in authority?—According to the *Prayer for the President*, what three areas are critical to pray for?

8. What important points should we pray concerning our economy?—In the *Prayer Declaration for the Economy*, what are the main reasons brought before God as to why our economy needs to remain strong?—In this declaration, what different strategies of warfare prayer can you identify?

9. What has facilitated the moral downward spiral of this nation in the past thirty or so years ?—According to Rev. Dutch Sheets, what is the decisive battle which will determine if we will win the war to save our nation?—What is the only way we can win this battle?—Identify the various names/titles of God used in the *Prayer Declaration for the Judicial System*. The many names that God has identified Himself by throughout Scripture are filled with *Covenant promises. Therefore, as intercessors we MUST call upon the name(s) of the Lord often!*

10. Who ultimately controls our national security?—What must be the stance of the intercessor when praying for God to protect this nation from disaster? "We must face the possibility that_____

_____

_____."

11. How does the sovereignty of God fit into this scenario? "We must make room for a merciful God to do _____

_____to effect change."

12. What conceals much demonic control in the world?—How?—Since terrorists are manipulated by spiritual forces, what must be removed in order for these men to be brought to justice?—It is of utmost importance that intercessors understand that *prayer should **never call for the destruction of people, but for the destruction of the evil systems (such as Islam) that hold people in bondage.* (For example, see the prayers concerning terrorism in America and worldwide terrorism). God loves all people, and desires that all should come to repentance and salvation. (see 1 Timothy 2:4 and 2 Peter 3:9.) Hence, the closing prayer under this heading is for the deliverance and salvation of the terrorists.

13. What are two commonly held civil doctrines in this country that do not line up with the intentions of the Constitution writers?—What serious perversions of justice have arisen to become laws of the land?— What is *true* liberty, according to Rev. Peter Marshall?—What is God's *alignment* in families; that is, what are the roles of children, husbands and wives toward each other according to God's Word? (See Ephesians 6:1-4 and Ephesians 5:21, 22 and 25.)

So I sought for a man among them who would make a wall, and stand in the gap before Me on behalf of the land, that I should not destroy it.

Ezekiel 22:30

CHALLENGE

Reread this chapter, and ask the Lord to give you a prayer burden for one of the targeted areas (the President, the economy, the judicial system, national security, terrorism, families or youth—or some other)

- *Prayer:* Then begin to incorporate this intercession into your daily prayers. In time, expand on the sample prayer in the book, or write your own decree or scriptural prayer for the area you chose (*see below). Incorporate as many scriptures and names of God as you can.
- *Action:* Look for opportunities to put "feet" to your prayers, such as helping with a youth ministry or pregnancy care center, or going to your state capital to visit your legislators.

*Keep in mind that political situations are continually in a state of flux. Look for signs of change and incorporate them into your intercession. For example, since *Praying With Authority and Power* was written, the situation in the U.S. has undergone change. There are subtle signs that the nation is beginning to turn toward God, and we need to keep our intercession current with the situation in our country. In view of this, I have written an updated version of the *Prayer for the United States.* This version reflects what God has done since the late summer/fall (2004) to begin to turn the nation. It also incorporates some insight garnered from Bill Lewis and his book, *The Sons of Issachar for the 21st Century,** about understanding the times through studying history in the context of Scripture.

Notice particular updates regarding:
- *recognizing God's mercy* and responding with repentance

- the *Pilgrims*: renew their original vision for America and their understanding of, and call to, *Israel*
- rebuilding the *altar of prayer*
- the call of President Bush as a *Hezekiah* leader (King Hezekiah initiated the longest revival in Israel's history: 130 years.) and as a *Cyrus* to Israel (Cyrus was used by God to release the Jews to return to their Zion, their Promised Land)
- adding the word "reformation" at the end, along with revival. *Reformation* (or a changed society) is what we really need. *Revival* will get us there!

REVISED PRAYER OVER AMERICA

Father, we thank You for the mercy and grace that You have extended to this nation, though we have been a stiff-necked and rebellious people who have run after other gods. Being men-pleasers instead of God-pleasers, we have lusted after pleasures, money, fame and power. Sexual irresponsibility and perversion have polluted our nation, and the blood of the innocents cries out to You. Our sins have destroyed lives, dishonored You, and defiled our land. Though we deserve judgment, O Lord, You have given us mercy instead of wrath (see Habakkuk 3:2). *May America recognize Your merciful hand, and respond with godly sorrow that brings forth repentance and righteousness* (see 2 Corinthians 7:10). *Holy Spirit, move upon the Church in America with a spirit of conviction so that God's people will humble themselves, and pray, and seek Your face, and turn from their wicked ways, so You can continue to turn this nation from destruction, forgive our sin, and heal our land* (2 Chronicles 7:14). *Father, reestablish justice as the measuring line and righteousness as the plumb line* (see Isaiah 28:17). *May America once again be a nation that is exalted by righteousness* (Proverbs 14:34) *and whose God is the Lord* (Psalm 33:12).

Lord, we bring You in remembrance of the blood of the martyrs upon this land—and of our godly heritage.... Lord, remember the faith of our founding fathers, and their holy covenant with You for the dedication of this land to the glory of God and the Gospel of the Lord Jesus Christ. Renew and reestablish their belief in America as a:

Community of Covenant believers, where the nations of the world come to be reconciled with God.

Blessing to Israel as God's chosen people, whose Covenant and destiny we share.

Place of refuge for the oppressed, the persecuted and the lost

O Lord, do not forget or forsake this Covenant, we pray. For the sake of Your mighty name, do not allow our enemies to triumph over us! Your Word says that when the enemy comes in like a flood, the Spirit of the Lord lifts up a standard against him (see Isaiah 59:19). Lord, we pray that You would raise a standard of repentance and righteousness across this land, so that the Redeemer will come to those who turn from transgression (see Isaiah 59:19-20). Uncap the wells of revival and let them gush forth with rivers of living water across this land.— Lord, SEND YOUR RAIN!—Soften the hardness of our hearts so the seeds You have sown can bring forth the fruit of righteousness in Your backslidden Church. (See Luke 8:15 and Psalm 72:6-7.) May the spirit of intercession and evangelism of Jonathan Edwards, Dwight L. Moody and Charles Finney be released upon us once again. Sovereign Lord, **rebuild the altar of prayer** in this nation:

May the Church come together in the spirit of unity of John 17:21, purifying the temple through holy worship and prayer.
May civil leaders stand in the posture of authority and pray God's heart over this land.
May You raise up a righteous remnant who will humble themselves before You and stand in the gap for this nation.

We lift up President Bush and ask that You give him a revelation of his calling as a **"Hezekiah" leader,** one who will lead this nation into revival, and as a **"Cyrus to Israel,"** one who will restore Israel to her Covenant Land. Lord, give him the courage, anointing and wisdom to step into this calling. May the **spirit of Hezekiah** flood this land and bring the people in remembrance of Your Covenant—And may remem-

brance produce repentance, renewal and a return to GOD. You said, Lord, that when we return to You, You will heal our backsliding (see Jeremiah 3:22). *May America turn to You with all of our heart with fasting, weeping and mourning* (see Joel 2:12).—*Turn us and heal us!—And shake the earth so that the ungodly structures of men may be removed, and Your Kingdom, which cannot be shaken, will remain* (see Hebrews12:26-28).

We declare over America that the LORD *is our Judge, the* LORD *is our Lawgiver, the* LORD *is our King HE will save us"* (Isaiah 33:22). *Will You not REVIVE us once again, that Your people may rejoice in You? (Psalm 85:6).*

Oh, do not remember the former iniquities against us! Let Your tender mercies come speedily to meet us... Restore us, O God of our salvation.... For Your name's sake! Why should the nations say, "Where is their God?" (Psalm 79:8-10)

Father, we pray for a mighty outpouring of Your Holy Spirit to bring forth REVIVAL and reformation and a great harvest of souls into this land. May Your River of Life be released to counter the "culture of death" which has gripped this nation.—And may America fulfill her God-ordained destiny in the earth.—In Jesus' name and to His glory!

---

*Bill Lewis, *The Sons of Issachar for the 21ˢᵗ Century—Understanding God's Heart for Our Times* (Xulon Press, June 30, 2004)

Chapter Eighteen: ISRAEL

1. Read Numbers 33:50 to 34:12, Ezekiel 47:13-20, and Genesis 15:18-21 to get an understanding of the land covenant *promised* to Israel by God as an *everlasting* inheritance (see Genesis 17:7-8).

   • First, note the boundaries of the covenant land, which extends roughly from the Sinai Peninsula near Egypt in the south, including Lebanon and into Syria in the north, and from the Mediterranean Sea in the west to the Euphrates River (Iraq) on the east.

   • Secondly, note God's command to "dispossess the inhabitants of the land and dwell in it, for I have given you the land to possess." If they didn't do this, the Lord said that "those whom you let remain shall be irritants in your eyes and thorns in your sides, and they shall harass you in the land where you dwell" (see Numbers 33:53 and 55).

Clearly, such areas as the "Gaza Strip," the "West Bank," and Jerusalem, all contested today, are Israel's by Covenant. Unfortunately, even most modern Israelis don't appreciate what is theirs by God's command, and so they have been duped into thinking that they can barter for peace by giving away land that is not theirs to give.—Do you think that God will allow His Covenant to be walked on and annulled by ignorant and greedy men?

2. Why does God command us to "pray for the peace of Jerusalem"? (This is the *only* city that He has ever made that command over.)

3. How can anything good come out of the terrorism and bloodshed in Israel today?—Why is it that the Jews, in general, cannot see the truth of the Messianic scriptures in the Old Testament?—How does understanding these things help us to pray?—Notice the different prayer strategies used in the decrees over Israel's Covenant land: closing spiritual doors with the *key of the house of David* (Isaiah 22:22), proclamation of the Word ("It is written..."), and the Blood of the Lamb.

4. What are the ancient roots of the "evil trinity" aligned against Israel from the north?—It is because these evil spiritual powers have no legal authority against Israel that we, as Blood-Covenant children of Almighty God, can take authority over them—through the Word, the Blood and the name of Jesus.

Notice the progression of the warfare in the decree against the "evil trinity":

- declaring that the Blood has triumphed
- calling upon the Lord to enforce His Word
- declaring the defeat of the enemy according to God's Word
- calling upon the Lord to bring righteous judgment
- declaring the supremacy of Christ and His Kingdom
- closing spiritual doors of access (according to Isaiah 22:22)
- declaring evil covenants annulled
- praising the Lord for victory!

5. What do Isaiah 48:1-11, Ezekiel 36:21-24, and Exodus 20:9 and 44 tell us about the Lord, and about Israel's ultimate destiny?

6. What does *covenant* mean?—Describe Israel's *covenantal relationship* with the Lord God.—What is God's promise in Ezekiel 36:21-24?—How does understanding these things give us confidence and faith to pray for the restoration of Israel?

7. With what we now understand, how can we approach God in intercession?—What are four points of strategic prayer that we can bring before the Lord in praying for Israel's spiritual and national restoration ?

CHALLENGE

Search your own heart for any anti-Semitic feelings you may have harbored, or any "Replacement Theology" (the belief that the Church has replaced Israel in God's redemptive/prophetic plan) teachings that you may have embraced, either through ignorance or through prejudice. Confess these to God and ask Him to give you *His* heart for Israel. If your church is one that embraces "Replacement Theology," pray for your pastor and leaders to have a true burden and love for Israel—and that God would give them revelation from His Word that He is shaping history for TWO groups of covenanted people: the Church *and* Israel.

Chapter Nineteen: THE NATIONS

1. "No matter what anti-God state the world is in today, God says that_____."

2. How do Jeremiah 1:9-10 and Matthew 6:10, instruct us regarding praying for the nations?

3. If Romans 13:1 is true, how do we account for evil leaders and tyrannical dictators such as Adolf Hitler and Saddam Hussein? (Read 1 Samuel 8:6-22 for clues.)—According to the *Prayer and Decree Over National Leaders*, what is the key scripture that should motivate the intercessor to pray for all national leaders— i.e., who is ultimately in control?

4. What false belief is at the root of Muslim intolerance?

5. What does history show us about the past and present influence of Islam on people and nations, both Muslim and non-Muslim?

6. Whom do Muslims trace their lineage to in Old Testament history?— What sin of Abraham and Sarah is still affecting the world today?— What can we learn from their mistake?—Why was Ishmael rejected as the Covenant son?—That God blessed him anyway, indicates what about God's character? (Hint: What does "Ishmael" mean?)

7. How does Genesis 16:12 apply to the Arab/Muslim peoples of today?

8. What is at the root of the Muslims' hatred for Israel and for all those who support her?

9. How does the blasphemous Muslim decree that *Amighty God* has called them to kill all *infidels* give us strategy to pray?—What is the *burqa* symbolic of?—What are two major prayer targets for the intercessor in all of this, and who is the real enemy?

10. What is the danger associated with false worship?—According to Emmanuel Kure, how can we, through prayer and spiritual warfare, overcome this danger?

11. Notice the prayer strategies in the powerful *Decree Over the Spiritual Stronghold of Islam:*

- appealing to God, who is **ALL** MIGHTY
- establishing the intercessor's authority according to Scripture
- declaring that the power of Islam is destroyed, and its dominion uprooted, by the power of the Blood of the cross and the Word of the Lord. This annuls all false prayer and decrees failure to all manipulations of evil powers.
- using the *key of the house of David*
- decreeing the sovereignty of God over the nations and the powers of darkness—that it is HE who defeats and dismantles principalities and powers, and that Jesus Christ is ultimately victorious!

12. Why is learning about Afghanistan strategic to the intercessor?—Looking at the *Prayer Decree Over Afghanistan*, what are some points of prayer that intercessors can use to pray for nations in similar political and socio-economic upheaval?

13. What spiritual influences in Iraq's past continue to exert influence on that nation today?—What are the indications that the prayers of God's people are having an effect in this land of political, social and economic turmoil?—What does the Scripture say about who really has control in the situation, and how does this direct our prayers?—What is the stance of the intercessor in this scenario?—Read the *Decree Over Iraq* and identify the prayer targets and strategies used.

14. What facts of Sudan's history are strategic to knowing how to pray for that nation?—Explain the significance of the *Falashas.*—What will warfare intercession accomplish in this case?—Notice the "declaratory" stance in the *Prophetic Decree of Hope.* Rather than a petition, this is a faith *declaration* of God's intent.

15. What is significant—and unique—about the conflict in Ireland?—What are the prayer targets identified here?—What are the specific spiritual strongholds that are challenged in the decree over Ireland?—What descriptive and covenantal names of God are used in the decree?

16. What does "the Harvest" represent?—What are the two groups of people described in the parable of the wheat and the tares?—What insight do we get from the prophet Hosea about the Harvest concerning what is necessary for the seeds of the Harvest to bring forth the fruit?

17. What insight is the intercessor given in Luke 10:2-3?—What two things are we called to do?—Why is it an urgent hour to pray?—What are the three titles of God used in the *Prophetic Call to Bring in the Harvest* that describe His work related to the Harvest?

18. What two basic things are necessary for peace?—What insight does the modern-day parable of the geese give us, and what should our response be?

19. What is the foundational reason for the lack of peace in the world?— How does one experience peace according to Isaiah 32:17-19?—Where is that place of peace according to Haggai 2:9?—And how do these insights help the intercessor pray, as evidenced in the *Prophetic Call for Peace*?

20. How do the last two prophetic prayers (for the Harvest, and for World Peace) differ from the other decrees in this chapter?

CHALLENGE

Expanding on Luke 10:2-3:

*"The harvest truly is great, but the laborers are few; therefore **pray** the Lord of the harvest to send out laborers into His harvest. **Go** your way; behold, I send you out."*

Jesus instructs us here to do two things: "pray" and "do."

- First, commit to PRAY for the Harvest as the Lord leads. And ask Him to expand your vision of the Harvest. Remember, it is as close as your next-door neighbor!
- Secondly, read 1 Corinthians 3:5-9 and seek God as to what He is calling you to DO. Are you a *planter*, a *waterer* or a *reaper*? Actually, all believers are called to be "planters"; that is, we are not all called to preach, but we are called to *witness*. If you have never tried to witness to anyone before, now is the time! Ask God for boldness, and begin to look for opportunities to share the love of Jesus, why you believe His Gospel, and how He has blessed your life. If you have experience in witnessing, renew your commitment to watch for those whom God brings across your path.

Chapter Twenty: BUILDING FAITH

1. Why is it impossible to please God without faith?—What is the connection between faith and the promises of God?

2. How can R. C. Sproul's interpretation of Hebrews 11:1 be applied to your life?

3. What strategy does the enemy use most often to tear down our faith?—What effect does this have on us, and what is the antidote?

4. How does fear affect our productivity?—"Courage is fear that _____."

5. According to 1 John 5:4: "This is the victory that _____
   _____the world— our _____."

6. "_____ is in our spiritual DNA."—What does Revelation
   3:21 tell us about faith and Heaven?

7. Discuss/meditate on the eight things highlighted on pages 196-97 that
   God desires to do in the lives of His children, and let these truths encourage your faith.

8. How does God sometimes use satan to benefit Believers?

9. What is a good way to build faith according to Romans 10:17?

CHALLENGE

Since faith is built up by *hearing* the Word of God, read the *Faith Builders* out loud each day and stretch your faith by *expecting* to see results!

Think of something that you have struggled with believing God for. Search the Scriptures to find a related promise you can stand on in prayer. And then *DECIDE to take God at His Word!*

Chapter Twenty-one: PERSONAL PRAYERS

1. What does Leonard Ravenhill's statement "People who are not praying are playing" mean to you?—According to Mr. Ravenhill, what two "prerequisites of dynamic Christian living" are generated in the prayer closet?—After reading his thoughts on prayer, do you have a better understanding of the state of the Church today?

2. Why are the psalms good models for prayer?—Look through the book of Psalms in your Bible and notice how many were written by David.—Does this give you some idea why God called David "a man after His own heart"? (1 Samuel 13:14).

3. What are the two main influences that operate to weaken our faith?

4. Personalize the *Binding and Loosing* prayer on page 207 to fit your needs and use this often in your personal intercession.

5. What is essential for Believers to experience the full victory of the life of faith?—What does the Bible say is the main reason God created man?—How does this make you feel?—Consider your life and how it would be if you didn't know God.

6. Can you think of other ways to resist the enemy besides the method highlighted?

7. What does Isaiah 53:4-5 provide for Believers?—How do we appropriate these promises into our lives?—How does Psalm 92:12-14 change your perspective on aging?—How does the sovereignty of God relate to healing?—What important conditions does Psalm 103:17-18 list as necessary in order to receive the Covenant promises of God?

8. How can understanding the Covenant promises of God make one a better intercessor?—What are the Covenant promises as summarized in Psalm 103:2-5?

KEY SCRIPTURE

"No weapon formed against you shall prosper, and every tongue which rises against you in judgment you shall condemn. This is the heritage of the servants of the LORD, and their righteousness is from Me," says the LORD.   Isaiah 54:17

CHALLENGE

Read Revelation 2:7, 11, 17, 26 and 28; 3:5, 12 and 21; and 21:7 to see the rewards of *overcomers.* How does this revelation motivate you to overcoming faith? Make the *Daily Confessions of an Overcomer* (on pages 204-205) a regular part of your personal intercession. Keep in mind that an "overcomer" is one who *overcomes* temptation, discouragement, fear, doubt, pride and all other demands and weaknesses of the flesh. To *overcome* is to face "the world, the flesh and the devil" head on and be victorious! And how do we overcome?—by the Blood of the Lamb and word of our testimony. (Revelation 12:11).

Chapter Twenty-two: PRAYING FOR OTHERS

1. What is the hardest mission field?—Why?—Why can we pray with great faith anyway?

2. What is the principle behind the life-changing power of the blessing?—What does the blessing impart?—What is the key to praying for children or others with special needs or problems?—Using the examples of the new job blessing and the marriage blessing, if you have children or grandchildren, think of ways you can bless them.

3. What effect can sin and iniquity have on the land? ... in the spirit?... and on future generations living on the land?

4. Where does the Believer's overcoming authority over the devil come from?

5. What three things does the Blood of Christ give us victory over?

6. From the perspective of spiritual warfare, what does the Blood of the Covenant provide for Believers?

7. Identify the strategic spiritual warfare operations (and scriptures) useful in cleansing defilement from land or property.

8. After reading the Epilogue, what is your answer to the final question: "Will you be one of them?"

And they overcame him [the devil] *by the blood of the Lamb and by the word of their testimony, and they did not love their lives to the death.*   Revelation 12:11

CHALLENGE

God told Abraham: "I will bless you … and *you shall be a blessing.*" (Genesis 12:2)

Jesus said: "Love your enemies, *bless those who curse you,* do good to those who hate you, and pray for those who spitefully use you and persecute you, *that you may be sons of your Father in heaven.*" (Matthew 5:44-45)

To close out this study on a positive note, think about how you can demonstrate the character and love of God your Father by being a *blessing* to the world around you:

- Re-read the "new job" and "marriage" blessings and then consider how you can bless someone close to you. - Not just in doing a kindness to them, but speaking a Scriptural blessing over them.

- When someone curses you or lashes out against you for any reason, develop a habit of "turning the other cheek" and blessing them instead of returning the insult.

- Thank the Lord every day for blessing you and ask Him to help you be a blessing to others.

Printed in the USA
CPSIA information can be obtained
at www.ICGtesting.com
LVHW092250311023
762732LV00028B/297